JOHANN
SEBASTION
BARK
LIVE

Other Piccolo Joke and Puzzle Books you will enjoy

The Blue Peter Book of Limericks Ed Biddy Baxter & Rosemary Gill

The Six Million Dollar Cucumber E. Richard Churchill

The Piccolo Book of Riddles S. B. Cunningham

Piccolo Book of Jokes Margaret Gosset

Silly Joke Book Stoo Hample

Sick as a Parrot: The World's Worst Jokes Nigel Blundell

The Absolute End: Some More of the World's Nutty News Stories Nigel Blundell and Robin Corry

Worst Jokes Nigel Blundell

We Are The Champions Jan Needle

Dotty Definitions Peter Eldin

The Cryptic Library by Rowan Barnes-Murphy

Ghosts, Ghouls and Bones

Vexed Vampires

Monstrous Mysteries

Muddled Mummies

Alien Antics

Witches, Wizards and Warlocks

The Riddler's Dictionary

compiled by
Peter Eldin

illustrated by
Jez Alborough

A Piccolo Original
Piccolo Books

First published 1985 by Pan Books Ltd,
Cavaye Place, London SW10 9PG

9 8 7 6 5 4 3

ISBN 0 330 28951 9

Photoset by Parker Typesetting Service, Leicester
Printed and bound in Great Britain by
Cox & Wyman Ltd, Reading

Contents

Riddler's dictionary A to C

Accident

Wife: Did you know most accidents happen in the kitchen?
Husband: Yes, I have to eat them.

Aeroplane

Q: Who invented the first aeroplane that didn't fly?
A: The Wrong Brothers.

Angry

Q: Why is it popular to be angry?
A: It's all the rage.

Animals

Q: What sort of animals use nut-crackers?
A: Toothless squirrels.

Army

Q: How do you join the army?
A: Tie the soldiers together.

Astronaut

Q: Where would an astronaut leave his spaceship?
A: At a parking meteor.

Authors

Q: Why are authors weird?
A: Because their tales come out of their heads.

•

Baby

Mother: Darling, why did you drop the baby?
Daughter: Well, you said he was a bonny bouncing baby and I wanted to see if it was true.

Baby astronaut

Q: How do you get a baby astronaut to sleep?
A: You rock-et.

Ballet

Q: Who plays in Trafalgar Square and dances at Covent Garden?
A: Dame Margot Fountain.

Bank

Careers Master: Why do you want to work in a bank?
Pupil: I'm told there's money in it.

Battery

Q: Why did the idiot bury his car battery?
A: He was told it was dead.

●

Bell

Q: What is brown and sounds like a bell?
A: Dung!

Book

Q: Who wrote 'Great Eggspectations'?
A: Charles Chickens.

Bulb

Q: What did the light bulb say to the switch?
A: You turn me on.

Burglar

Q: Why did the burglar have a bath?
A: He wanted to make a clean getaway.

Bury St Edmunds

Fred: I'm going to Bury St Edmunds today.
Freda: I didn't even know he was dead.

Butcher's boy

Q: What do you call a butcher's boy?
A: A chop assistant.

•

Candle

Q: What did the boy candle say to the girl candle?
A: Let's go out together.

•

Car

Q: What happens to German cars when they get old?
A: They go to an old Volks home.

Cat

Q: What do cats read?
A: Mewspapers.

Centipede

Q: What did one centipede say to the other centipede as a lady centipede walked past?
A: There's a lovely pair of legs, pair of legs, pair of legs, pair of legs . . .

Chiropodist

Q: What does a chiropodist have for breakfast?
A: Corn-flakes.

Cleaner

Q: What's an office cleaner's favourite dance?
A: The char-char.

Cloakroom attendant

Q: What do you call a Scottish cloakroom attendant?
A: Angus McCoatup.

Clock

Q: How did you manage to buy that expensive clock?
A: I got it on tick.

Concorde

Q: As Concorde flew over, one bird said to the other, 'Gee, I wish I could fly as fast as that.'
A: The second bird said, 'You would if your bottom was on fire like that!'

Cook

Q: Who's a cook's favourite composer?
A: Ludwig Van Bakeoven.

Cow

Q: What would you get if you walked under a cow?
A: A pat on the head.

•

Signs of the times

Admiral's door

Gone to launch.

At the top of an idiot's ladder

Stop.

Beekeeper's door

Back in hive minutes.

Butcher's shop

Pleased to meet you, meat to please you.

Cleaners

We'll clean for you. We'll press for you. We'll even dye for you.

Dairy

You can whip our cream but you can't beat our milk.

Egyptologist

Satisfaction guaranteed or your mummy back.

Fortune teller

Closed owing to unforeseen circumstances.

Golf club clubroom

Back soon. Gone to tee.

•

Hairdresser's

We curl up and dye for you.

Health food shop

Closed due to illness.

Jeweller's window

Ears pierced while you wait.

Pet shop

In the interest of dogs, hygiene is not permitted in this shop.

Psychiatrist

Satisfaction guaranteed or your mania back.

Restaurant

Eat now – pay waiter.

Road sign

When this sign is under water, the road is closed to traffic.

Sheriff's door

Gone to lynch.

Stationery shop

Calendars and diaries.
All with one year's guarantee.

Travel agent

Please go away.

•

Doctor, doctor

Apple

Patient: Is it true that an apple a day keeps the doctor away?
Nurse: Yes it is.
Patient: Well, give me an apple quick. I've just broken the doctor's window.

Cabbages

Patient: Doctor, doctor, I've got cabbages growing out of my ears!
Doctor: My goodness, I've no idea how that happened.
Patient: Neither have I – I planted broad beans.

Coffee

Patient: Doctor, doctor, I feel like a weak coffee.
Doctor: So do I, go and make me one.

Cold

Patient: Doctor, how can I prevent this head cold going down to my chest?
Doctor: Tie a knot in your neck.

Dog

Patient: Doctor, my brother thinks he's a dog.
Doctor: How long has this been going on?
Patient: Ever since he was a puppy.

•

Dustbin

Patient: Doctor, doctor, I feel like a dustbin.
Doctor: Don't talk rubbish.

Eyes

Doctor: When did you last have your eyes checked?
Patient: Never. They've always been blue.

Film

Patient: Doctor, doctor, I've just swallowed a roll of film.
Doctor: Don't worry. Just wait and see what develops.

Insects

Patient: Doctor, what is the best way to prevent illnesses caused by biting insects?
Doctor: Don't bite any insects.

Invisible man

Q: What did the doctor say to the Invisible Man?
A: I'm sorry but I can't see you today.

Liar

Patient: Doctor, doctor, everyone thinks I'm a liar.
Doctor: I don't believe that.

Liver

Patient: Doctor, doctor, have you got something for my liver?
Doctor: How about some onions?

Marshmallow

Patient: Doctor, doctor, last night I dreamed I had eaten a monster marshmallow.
Doctor: Don't worry, it was only a dream.
Patient: Maybe, but when I woke up my pillow had gone!

Milk

Boy: My mum's doctor recommended that she bathes in milk.
Girl: And does she?
Boy: No, she can't get into the bottle.

Nose

Patient: Doctor how do I stop my nose from running?
Doctor: Put your foot out and try to trip it up.

Pills

Boy: My doctor told me to take two of these pills on an empty stomach.
Girl: Did they do any good?
Boy: No, they kept rolling off.

Pipe

Patient: Doctor, doctor, why do I feel like a pipe sticking out of the back of a car?
Doctor: Because you're exhausted.

•

What an insult!

Age

She's so old, when she was was a girl Billy wasn't even a kid.

Baldness

That's the first time I've seen a parting with ears.

Birth

Your mother should have thrown you away and kept the stork.

Bore

You're like a drip – you can always hear it but you can't turn it off.

Brain

What does your brain want to be when it grows up?

Cook

Her cooking is so bad, pygmies come from Africa to dip their arrows in her food.

Ears

Your ears are so big you look like a car with the doors open.

Face

You've got the type of face you don't want to remember but can't forget.

Films

The trouble with most films is that they shoot too much film and not enough actors.

Fool

He is like a piece of blotting paper. He soaks everything in – but gets it all backwards.

Gossip

She talks so much that when she goes on holiday she spreads sunburn lotion on her tongue.

Hair

I'd like a lock of your hair – I'm stuffing a mattress.

Head

Don't scratch your head, you might get a splinter in your finger.

Hotel

The rooms are so small even the mice have got round shoulders.

Idea

Say, you've got something there – let's hope it isn't catching.

Inquisitiveness

He's so inquisitive he once took his nose apart to see what makes it run.

Job

He lost his last job through illness – the boss got sick of him.

Mean person

He's so mean that if he was a ghost he wouldn't give you a fright.

•

Memory

You've got a memory like an elephant – and a face to match.

Mind

He's going out of his mind – and his mind is glad he's leaving.

Moustache

His moustache and my dog go to the same vet.

Mouth

The last time I saw a mouth like that there was a fish hook in it.

Pianist

At his last performance the audience cheered and cheered. The piano was locked.

Restaurant

If this is coffee, please bring me some tea. But if this is tea, please bring me some coffee.

School

The kids at that school are so tough the teachers play truant.

Sense

You must have a sixth sense, because you show no sign of the other five.

Singer

His singing is improving. People are putting cotton wool in only one ear now.

Small person

He's so small, every time he gets toothache he thinks he's got a corn on his foot.

Stupid

I don't know what it is that makes you so stupid but whatever it is, it works.

Suit

That suit fits you like a glove. It's a pity it doesn't fit you likc a suit.

•

Teeth

Her teeth stick out so much it looks like her nose is playing the piano.

Thin person

He's so thin you could use him as a bookmark.

Tired person

He's rather tired. Last night he dreamed he was working.

•

Riddler's dictionary D to L

Dance

Have you heard about the new dance? It's called 'The Lift' because there are no steps in it.

Dictator

Q: Who was the strongest dictator?
A: Muscle-ini.

Dishwasher

Wife: Why don't we have an automatic dishwasher?
Husband: We don't have automatic dishes.

Dog

Q: Who's a dog's favourite composer?
A: Johann Sebastian Bark.

Duchess

Q: Have you seen a Duchess?
A: No, but I've seen an English s.

•

Ear

Q: Do you play the piano by ear?
A: No, I use my fingers.

Egg

Q: What do you call a mischievous egg?
A: A practical yolker.

Elephant

Q: Why are elephants wrinkled?
A: Have you ever tried ironing one?

Execution

On the day of his execution the convicted murderer was granted a last request.

'I'd like to sing a song,' said the condemned man.

'Certainly,' said the prison governor.

And the man began to sing, 'Nine hundred and ninety-nine thousand nine hundred and ninety-nine bottles, hanging on the wall . . .'

Eye

Q: What did one eye say to the other eye?
A: Between you and me, something smells.

•

Fire

The fire was raging as an harassed woman holding a baby appeared at a top storey window. 'Throw the baby down,' called a man on the ground.

'But you might drop him,' the woman screamed.

'No I won't,' replied the man, 'I'm a professional goalkeeper.'

Reassured by this remark the woman dropped the baby and was relieved to see the goalie catch it safely. Then he bounced it on the ground three times and kicked it over the hedge!

Fisherman

Q: What do fishermen use to eat Chinese take-away meals?
A: Ship sticks.

Flower

I had to stop wearing a flower in my button hole.
The flower pot kept hitting me in the stomach.

Food

Q: What's brown, tasty and stupid?
A: Thick soup.

Food

Q: What do computer experts have for tea?
A: Fish and microchips.

Fool

Q: Are you trying to make a fool out of me?
A: Oh no, I never interfere with nature.

Free speech

Boy: Do you believe in free speech?
Girl: Of course!
Boy: Good, can I use your telephone?

•

Garage mechanic

Q: Who was the garage mechanic's favourite artist?
A: Van go.

Gardener

Q: What is a gardener's favourite magazine?
A: Weeder's Digest.

Girlfriend

Q: Why do you call your girlfriend your 'melancholy baby'?
A: Because she's got a shape like a melon and a face like a collie.

Green

Q: What is green and goes boing, boing, boing?
A: A spring cabbage.

•

Hand

Fred: May I hold your hand?
Freda: No thanks, it isn't heavy.

Head

You have a good head on your shoulders – but it would look better on your neck.

Heads

Q: What has fifty heads but no hair?
A: A box of matches.

Hot dog

Q: What do you call a long hot-dog?
A: A frankfurther.

•

Idiot

Q: What do you mean by telling everyone I'm an idiot?
A: I'm sorry, I didn't know it was a secret.

Indian

Q: What did Big Chief Running Water call his two children?
A: Hot and Cold.

Indicators

Q: Are my car indicators working?
A: Yes, no, yes, no, yes, no, yes, no, yes . . .

Invisible ink

Customer:	Have you any invisible ink?
Shop Assistant:	Yes, sir. What colour?

Irishman

Fred:	My sister married an Irishman.
Charlie:	Oh, really?
Fred:	No, O'Reilly.

•

James Watt

Q: What happened when James Watt saw steam coming from a kettle?
A: He discovered it was time to make the tea.

Judge

Q: What did the judge say when he finished work?
A: It's been another trying day.

Judicious

Teacher:	Give me a sentence with the word 'judicious' in it.
Pupil:	Hands that judicious can be soft as your face.

•

King Charles

Q: What was King Charles's last request before he was executed?
A: Can I take a walk around the block?

•

Litter

Q: How do you train a litter collector?
A: You don't – you just let him pick it up as he goes along.

Loan

Lend me five pence, I want to telephone a friend.
Here's ten pence, ring all of them.

Love

Girl: Darling, do you love me?
Boy: Of course I do.
Girl: Well, please say something soft and sweet to me.
Boy: Lemon meringue pie.

•

Did you hear?

Accident

Did you hear about the accident at the supermarket? A man was looking into the frozen food cabinet when five fish fingers reached out and strangled him.

Accountant

Did you hear about the accountant who had two chickens in his office? They helped him make hens meet.

Athlete

Did you hear why Russian athletes are so fast? Their starting guns contain real bullets.

Bird impressions

Did you hear about the schoolboy who does bird impressions? He eats worms.

Blood

Did you hear about the two blood corpuscles? They loved in vein.

Boy

Did you hear about the little boy who was named after his father? They called him Dad.

Boy Scout

Did you hear about the dizzy Boy Scout? He'd spent all day doing good turns.

Car

Did you hear about the car that couldn't play football? It only had one boot.

•

Cat

Did you hear that cats like to go to one place for their holidays? The Canary Islands.

Christening

Did you hear about the little boy called Glug-Glug? He was going to be christened Anthony but the vicar fell into the font.

Clock

Did you hear about the man who shot a clock? He said he was just killing time.

Comedian

Did you hear about the motorbike made especially for comedians? It's called a Yamaha-ha-ha.

Computer

Did you hear how you can beat a chess-playing computer? Use a hammer.

Cow

Did you hear about the cow who went out every evening? He went to the moo-vies.

Dolphin

Did you hear about the angry dolphins? They were at cross porpoises.

Fisherman

Did you hear about the deaf fisherman? He wore a herring aid.

Idiot

Did you hear about the idiot who kept saying 'no'?
No.
Ah, so it was you!

Indian

Did you hear about the fussy indian? He had reservations.

Marriage

Did you hear about the couple who were happily married? She was happy and he was married.

Mirror

Did you hear about the man who looked at the mirror with his eyes shut? He wanted to see what he looked like when he was asleep.

Nose

Did you hear about the boy with a turned-up nose? Every time he sneezed he blew his school cap off.

Optician

Did you hear about the optician's twins? They made a spectacle of themselves.

Paper shop

Did you hear about the man who bought a paper shop? It blew away.

Parrot

Did you hear about the parrot in prison? He was put in the polly-cell.

Plastic surgeon

Did you hear about the plastic surgeon who went sunbathing? He melted.

Pop star

Did you hear why pop stars always stay cool? They've got lots of fans.

Prisoner

Did you hear about the prisoner who was given a suspended sentence? They hanged him.

Sheepdog

Did you hear about the sheepdog trials? The sheepdogs were found not guilty.

•

Spanish lady

Did you hear about the Spanish lady who had identical twins? She couldn't tell Juan from the other.

Submarine

Did you hear about the man who was sacked from the submarine service? He was found sleeping on duty – with the windows open.

Sunglasses

Did you hear about the man who always wore sunglasses? He took a dim view of things.

Sword swallower

Did you hear about the sword swallower on a diet? He only eats knives and forks.

Tap dancer

Did you hear about the tap dancer who had an accident? He fell off the tap.

Thief

Did you hear about the thief who stole some elastic? He was put away for a long stretch.

Tree

Did you hear about the tree that grows in your hand? It's called a palm.

Turnip

Did you hear about the two turnips who were in love? They were swedehearts.

•

Witch

Did you hear about the witch who had identical twins? She couldn't tell which from which.

•

Animal crackers

Antelope

Why did the ant elope? Nobody gnu.

Ape

What do apes sing at Christmas? Jungle bells, jungle bells . . .

Bear

How do you start a bear race? Ready, teddy, go.

Bird

What do birds have for breakfast? Shredded tweet or tweet-a-bix.

Bison

What's the difference between a buffalo and a bison? You can't wash your hands in a buffalo.

Buffalo

How do you stop a herd of buffalo from charging? Take away their credit cards.

Camel

What do you call a camel with three humps? Humphrey.

Cat

What noise does a cat make on a motorway? Miaoooooooooooooow!

Cow

Q: What sort of cows do they have in the frozen north?
A: Eskimoos.

Dog

First dog: Woof woof.
Second dog: Miaow.
First dog: What do you mean 'miaow'?
Second dog: I'm learning a foreign language.

Dolphin

Dolphins are so clever that in just a few weeks in a dolphinarium they can train a man to stand on the edge of the pool and throw them fish three times a day.

•

Duck

Q: What TV programmes do ducks like?
A: Duckumentaries.

Elephant

Q: Why were the elephants the last to leave the Ark?
A: They had to pack their trunks.

Flea

Q: How do you start a flea race?
A: Say one, two, flea . . . go.

Frog

Q: What did the vet do to the sick frog?
A: Gave it an hoperation.

Geese

Q: What do geese eat?
A: Gooseberries.

Gnu

Q: Why did the zookeeper separate the gnus?
A: Because he had some good gnus and some bad gnus.

Gorilla

Q: What would you do if a large gorilla sat in front of you at the cinema?
A: Miss most of the film.

Hippopotamus

Q: How do you know there's a hippopotamus under your bed?
A: Your face is pressing against the ceiling.

Horse

Q: How do you make a slow racehorse fast?

A: Don't give him any food.

•

Jelly fish

Did you hear about the stupid jelly fish? It set.

Kangaroo

Q: What's a kangaroo's favourite TV programme?

A: Dr. Roo.

Ladybird

Boy: You shouldn't have trodden on that ladybird, they're lucky.
Girl: That one wasn't.

Octopus

Q: What did the boy octopus say to the girl octopus?
A: I want to hold your hand, hand, hand, hand, hand, hand, hand, hand.

Pig

Q: What would happen if pigs could fly?
A: Bacon would go up.

Ram

Q: What did the ram say to his girlfriend?
A: I love ewe.

Rhinoceros

Q: What do you give a seasick rhinoceros?
A: Lots of room.

Sardine

Q: What did the baby sardine say to the mother sardine as a submarine passed by?
A: Look at that can of people.

Sheep

Q: How do sheep keep warm?
A: Central bleating.

Skunk

Q: Why is a skunk in the room like a house on fire?
A: The sooner you put it out the better.

Stoat

Q: Why did the two American stoats get married?
A: They wanted to be the United Stoats of America.

Toad

Q: How did the toad cross the Channel?
A: By hopper-craft.

•

Grub up

Apple

Q: What is worse than finding a maggot in the apple you are eating?
A: Finding half a maggot.

Bean

Q: What is this?
A: It's bean soup.
Q: I don't care what it's been, what is it now?

Bread

Customer: This slice of bread is tough!
Waiter: No wonder. You're eating the paper plate!

Breakfast

Q: What do centipedes have for breakfast?
A: Feetabix.

Cake

Q: Mum, can I have two pieces of cake, please?
A: Certainly, take this piece and cut it in two.

Chicken

Customer: Waiter! This chicken is terrible! Bring me the manager.
Waiter: Sorry sir, but he's not on the menu.

Chicken soup

Wife: I've made the chicken soup.
Husband: Good. I thought it was for me.

Coffee

Q: Is that coffee I smell?
A: It is and you do.

Duck

Q: Do you like duck?
A: Duck is my favourite chicken, except for turkey.

Egg

Q: What is the difference between an egg and a mare?
A: An egg is E GG and a mare is SHE GG.

Fish and chips

A man walked into a fish shop and said, 'Fish and chips, twice.' 'I heard you the first time,' said the woman behind the counter.

Honey

Mother: Why do you keep putting honey on your knife?
Caroline: It stops the peas rolling off.

Milk pudding

Q: How do you start a milk pudding race?
A: Sago.

Pea

Mother: Caroline, you know you shouldn't eat peas with your knife.
Caroline: I know, but my fork leaks.

Pie

Q: What pie can fly?
A: A magpie.

Plum

Q: How can you measure the colour of plums?
A: Use a green gauge.

Pork

Waiter: How did you find your pork chop, sir?
Customer: I just lifted a chip and there it was.

•

Potato

Q: What vegetable goes best with jacket potatoes?
A: Button mushrooms.

•

Sauce

Q: Why did the tomato sauce chase the brown sauce?
A: It was trying to ketchup.

Sausages

Q: What's the best day for eating sausages?
A: Fry-day.

Spaghetti

Q: How long do you cook spaghetti?
A: About ten inches.

Steak

Q: How does a lion like his steak cooked?
A: Medium roar.

Sweet

Q: What's a pilot's favourite sweet?
A: Plain chocolate.

Turkey

Q: Where do good turkeys go when they die?
A: To oven.

•

Riddler's dictionary M to S

M

Q: Why should you never put the letter *M* into a fridge?
A: Because it changes 'ice' into 'mice'.

Magic

Q: Which magician cries the most?
A: Bawl Daniels.

Magician

Q: Who is the noisiest magician?
A: Paul Dan Yells.

Magnet

Q: What did the boy magnet say to the girl magnet?
A: I find you very attractive.

Match

Charlie: This match won't light.
Fred: That's unusual.
Charlie: Yes, it worked last time I tried it.

Me

Q: If I had three noses, six eyes and two mouths, what would I be?
A: Ugly.

Miner

Q: What is a miner's favourite game?
A: Mineopoly.

Miser

Q: What is a miser's favourite game?
A: Meanopoly.

Misers

Q: How do misers keep warm when it's cold?
A: They sit around a candle.
Q: How do misers keep warm when it's very cold?
A: They light it.

Misery

Q: What is a miserable person's favourite game?
A: Moanopoly.

Morris

Q: What happened to your Morris car?
A: Morris took it back.

Motor car hooter

Q: Where do the Chinese make motor car hooters?
A: Hong King.

Music

Q: Where does a bad choir go for its holiday?
A: Singapore.

•

Nose

Q: How did you manage to break your nose?
A: Do you see that lamp-post?
Q: Yes.
A: Well I didn't.

•

Ocean

Q: What do you call someone who crosses an ocean twice without having a bath?
A: A dirty double crosser.

Newspaper

Q: Why is a newspaper better than a TV set?
A: You can't swot flies with a TV.

Orchestra

Q: What do you call it when a symphony orchestra holds up a bank?
A: Robbery with violins.

•

Paint

Q: Why did you paint your wife in oils?
A: Because she's got a face like a sardine.

Pet shop

Here is the news:

A local pet shop was burgled today. Police say they have not yet caught the burglar because there aren't any leads.

Piano

Q: Do you play the piano by ear?
A: No, I play it over there.

Pirate

Q: What did they call the pirate when his wooden leg broke?
A: Short John Silver.

Police

Here is the news:

The police are searching for a man with one eye called Jones.

They haven't said what the other eye is called.

Policeman

Q: Who was the policeman's favourite artist?
A: Constable.

•

Poor

We were so poor my parents couldn't afford to buy me shoes. I used to blacken my feet and lace my toes together.

Printer

Careers Master: Why do you want to be a printer?
Pupil: I think I'm the right type.

Prisoners

Here is the news:
Two prisoners escaped today. One is very tall and the other is very short. Police are hunting high and low for them.

•

Race

Q: How do you start a jelly race?
A: On your marks, get set.

Reverse

Policeman: Why are you driving your car in reverse?
Motorist: Because I know the Highway Code backwards.

Ringleader

Q: What is a ringleader?
A: The first person in the bath.

Roman

Q: Why is the letter P like a Roman emperor?
A: Because it is near O.

Ruler

Q: Why did the idiot take a ruler to bed?
A: He wanted to see how long he slept.

Runner

Here is the news:

The famous runner Arthur Letix ran for twenty minutes today but moved only two feet. That's all he's got.

•

Sea

Girl: You remind me of the sea.
Boy: Why? Because I'm wild, exciting and romantic?
Girl: No, you just make me sick.

Shoulder

Girl: What's that ugly thing on your shoulder?
Boy: I don't know. What is it?
Girl: Your head!

Singer

Q: When is a bad singer like a pirate?
A: When it's murder on the high C's.

Sledge

Girl: Can I share your sledge?
Boy: Certainly, we'll go halves.
Girl: Gee, that is sure nice of you.
Boy: I'll have it for downhill and you can have it for uphill.

Smile

Keep smiling. It makes everybody wonder what you are up to.

Sons

Q: Why did the parents name both of their sons Edward?
A: Because two Eds are better than one.

Spiders

Q: Where do spiders play football?
A: Webley.

Sponge

Q: What holds water and yet is full of holes?
A: A sponge.

Strike

Boy: The men in the factory are striking for shorter hours.
Girl: Good. I've always thought sixty minutes was too long for an hour.

Suitcase

Q: What's brown and carries a suitcase?
A: A handle.

Sums

Q: What sea creature is good at sums?
A: An octoplus.

•

Cross purposes

Batman

Q: What do you get if you cross Batman and Robin with a steamroller?
A: Flatman and Ribbon.

Bell

Q: What do you get if you cross a bell with a monster ape?
A: A ding-dong King Kong.

Budgerigar

Q: What do you get if you cross a budgerigar with a lawnmower?
A: Shredded tweet.

Cocoa bean

Q: What do you get if you cross a cocoa bean with an elk?
A: A chocolate moose.

Comedian

Q: What do you get if you cross a comedian with an oxo cube?
A: A laughing stock.

•

Cowboy

Q: What do you get if you cross a cowboy with a tasty meal?
A: Hoppalong casserole.

Detective

Q: What do you get if you cross a famous detective with some elves?
A: Sherlock Gnomes.

Dictionary

Q: What do you get if you cross a dictionary with an insect?
A: A spelling bee.

Dog

Q: What do you get if you cross a dog with a cat?
A: An animal that chases itself.

Father Christmas

Q: What do you get if you cross Father Christmas with a detective?
A: Santa Clues.

Goat

Q: What do you get if you cross a goat with a nosey man?
A: Someone who is always butting into other people's business.

Fish

Q: What do you get if you cross a fish with an elephant?
A: Swimming trunks.

Holiday

Q: What do you get if you cross a holiday with two newly-wed rabbits?
A: A bunnymoon.

Magician

Q: What do you get if you cross a magician with a whale?
A: Moby Trick.

Mint

Q: What do you get if you cross a mint sweet with a grizzly?
A: A polo bear.

Monkey

Q: What do you get if you cross a monkey with a flower?
A: A chimp-pansy.

Pig

Q: What would you get if you crossed a pig with a telephone?
A: Crackling on the line.

Plumber

Q: What do you get if you cross a plumber with a doctor?
A: A drain surgeon.

Policeman

Q: What do you get if you cross a bald policeman with a camera?
A: A Kojak Instamatic.

•

Porcupine

Q: What do you get if you cross a porcupine with a mole?
A: A tunnel that leaks.

Rabbit

Q: What do you get if you cross a rabbit with a leek?
A: A bunion.

Shark

Q: What do you get if you cross a shark with a playright?
A: Jaws Bernard Shaw.

Snake

Q: What do you get if you cross a snake with a window of a motor car?
A: A windscreen viper.

Whale

Q: What do you get if you cross a whale with a goose?
A: Moby Duck.

Wine

Q: What do you get if you cross a bottle of wine with an African animal?
A: A wine-oceros.

•

Wool

Q: What do you get if you cross a ball of wool, with two needles and a comedian?
A: A knit-wit.

•

What's the difference?

Athlete

Q: What's the difference between an athlete and a duck?
A: One is quick on two legs, the other is quack on two legs.

Comedian

Q: What's the difference between a comedian and a forger?
A: One makes the funny and the other fakes the money.

Dog

Q: What's the difference between a flea-bitten dog and a bored guest?
A: One is going to itch and the other is itching to go.

Fish

Q: What's the difference between a fish and a piano?
A: You can't tuna fish.

Gardener

Q: What's the difference between a gardener and a snooker player?
A: One minds his peas, the other minds his cues.

Hill

Q: What's the difference between a hill and a pill?
A: A hill is hard to get up and a pill is hard to get down.

Horse

Q: What's the difference between a sick horse and a dead bee?
A: One is a seedy beast, the other is a bee deceased.

Iceberg

Q: What's the difference between an iceberg and a clothes brush?
A: One crushes boats and the other brushes coats.

Kangaroo

Q: What's the difference between a kangaroo and a lumberjack?
A: One hops and chews, the other chops and hews.

Photography

Q: What's the difference between photography and influenza?
A: One makes facsimiles, the other makes sick families.

Railway engine

Q: What's the difference between a railway engine and a tree?
A: One leaves its shed, the other sheds its leaves.

Tree

Q: What's the difference between an oak tree and a tight shoe?
A: One makes acorns and the other makes corns ache.

Robber

Q: What's the difference between a robber and a church bell?
A: One steals from the people, the other peels from the steeple.

Riddler's dictionary T to Z

T

Q: What starts with T, ends with T, and has T in it?
A: A teapot.

Table

Salesman: This table is in mint condition.
Customer: Yes, I can see – it's got a hole in the middle.

Tap

Q: What did the little tap say to the big tap?
A: You big drip!

Telephone

Boy: Answer the telephone.
Girl: It's not ringing.
Boy: Why do you have to leave everything to the last minute?

Thief

Q: What do you call a motorcycle thief?
A: A Honda-taker.

Time

Q: How can you tell the time with a candle?
A: Listen to the candles-tick.

Toe

Q: What did one big toe say to the other big toe?
A: Don't look now, but there's a couple of heels following us.

Tower of Pisa

Q: What made the Tower of Pisa lean?
A: A strict diet.

Train

Q: Why did the train stop half-way across the prairie?
A: It had injun trouble.

Travel

Q: How did David Frost get to work?
A: By icicle.

Trifle

Q: Who was the trifle's favourite artist?
A: Bottijelli.

Trousers

Q: Why are you wearing drainpipe trousers?
A: I've got water on the knee.

Twins

Boy: My girlfriend is one of twins.
Girl: Can you tell them apart?
Boy: Oh yes, her brother has a beard.

•

Umbrella

Q: Why do businessmen carry umbrellas?
A: Because umbrellas can't walk.

Undertaker

Q: How can you distinguish an undertaker?
A: By his grave manner.

Urn

Q: What's a Grecian urn?
A: About £60 a week.

•

Vet

Q: What does the vet give a sick bird?
A: Tweetment.

Video

Mrs Idiot wanted a video recorder but Mr Idiot said they could not afford one.

The following day Mrs Idiot staggered into the house with a brand-new video.

'Where on earth did you get the money to buy that?' gasped Mr Idiot.

'That's easy,' said Mrs Idiot, 'I sold the television.'

•

Waiter

Q: What did the waiter do when a lady fainted in the restaurant?
A: He gave her the quiche of life.

Wart

Q: Who's the lady with the wart?
A: That's her husband.

Washing line

Q: What goes at 100 m.p.h. along a washing line?
A: Honda pants.

Water

Q: When is water musical?
A: When it's piping hot.

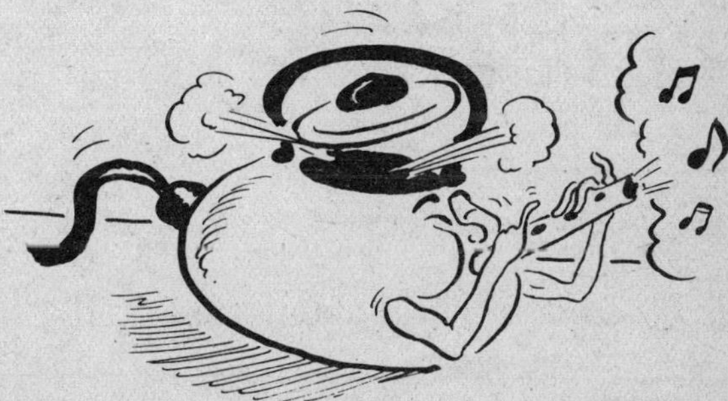

Wife

Fred: I wish I had my wife back.
Charlie: Where is she?
Fred: I swapped her for a video recorder.
Charlie: And now you realise how much you love her?
Fred: No. Now I want a home computer.

Witch

Q: Why does a witch ride on a broom?
A: Because a vacuum cleaner is too heavy.

Woman

Q: What do you call a wicked woman who lives by the sea?
A: A sandwitch.

Woodworm

Q: Did you hear about the stupid woodworm?
A: It died in a brick.

Zebra crossing

Policeman: Why are you crossing the road at this busy spot? Can't you see there's a zebra crossing just up the road?

Pedestrian: Well, I hope he's having more luck than I am.

Knock, knock

Alison

Knock, Knock.
Who's there?
Alison.
Alison who?
Alison to the radio.

Annie

Knock, Knock.
Who's there?
Annie.
Annie who?
Annie one going to open this door?

Atch

Knock, Knock.
Who's there?
Atch.
Atch who?
That's a bad cold you've got.

Bertha

Knock, Knock.
Who's there?
Bertha.
Bertha who?
Bertha day greetings.

Canoe

Knock, Knock.
Who's there?
Canoe.
Canoe who?
Canoe come out to play?

Cyril

Knock, Knock.
Who's there?
Cyril.
Cyril who?
Cyril pleasure to meet you.

Diana

Knock, Knock.
Who's there?
Diana.
Diana who?
Diana thirst, can I have a glass of water?

Diesel

Knock, Knock.
Who's there?
Diesel.
Diesel who?
Diesel teach you to answer the door.

Don

Knock, Knock.
Who's there?
Don.
Don who?
Don' just stand there, open the door.

Doris

Knock, Knock.
Who's there?
Doris.
Doris who?
Doris shut on my finger, open it quick.

Doughnut

Knock, Knock.
Who's there?
Doughnut.
Doughnut who?
Doughnut ask such silly questions.

Eddie

Knock, Knock.
Who's there?
Eddie.
Eddie who?
Eddie body in there?

Egbert

Knock, Knock.
Who's there?
Egbert.
Egbert who?
Egbert no bacon.

Europe

Knock, Knock.
Who's there?
Europe.
Europe who?
Europe early this morning.

Fozzie

Knock, Knock.
Who's there?
Fozzie.
Fozzie who?
Fozzie last time, let me in!

Freddie

Knock, Knock.
Who's there?
Freddie.
Freddie who?
Freddie or not, here I come.

Gerald

Knock, Knock.
Who's there?
Gerald.
Gerald who?
Gerald friend.

Goose

Knock, Knock.
Who's there?
Goose.
Goose who?
Goose who's knocking at your door?

Gutter

Knock, Knock.
Who's there?
Gutter.
Gutter who?
Gutter get in, that's why I'm knocking on the door.

Howard

Knock, Knock.
Who's there?
Howard.
Howard who?
Howard you know if you don't open the door?

Isadore

Knock, Knock.
Who's there?
Isadore.
Isadore who?
Isadore open or locked?

Juno

Knock, Knock.
Who's there?
Juno.
Juno who?
Juno who I am?

Kent

Knock, Knock.
Who's there?
Kent.
Kent who?
Kent you guess who it is?

Luke

Knock, Knock.
Who's there?
Luke.
Luke who?
Luke through the keyhole and you'll see.

Major

Knock, Knock.
Who's there?
Major.
Major who?
Major answer the door.

Olga

Knock, Knock.
Who's there?
Olga.
Olga who?
Olga home if you don't open the door.

Oswald

Knock, Knock.
Who's there?
Oswald.
Oswald who?
Oswald my chewing gum.

Owl

Knock, Knock.
Who's there?
Owl.
Owl who?
Owl you know unless you open the door?

Paul

Knock, Knock.
Who's there?
Paul.
Paul who?
Paul hard, the door's stuck.

Rupert

Knock, Knock.
Who's there?
Rupert.
Rupert who?
Rupert your right arm in, your right arm out . . .

Shirley

Knock, Knock.
Who's there?
Shirley.
Shirley who?
Shirley you know who I am?

Sid

Knock, Knock.
Who's there?
Sid.
Sid who?
Sid down and make yourself at home.

Theodore

Knock, Knock.
Who's there?
Theodore.
Theodore who?
Theodore is shut. Please let me in.